Nova S, 1975—

5237 · 8

© 1990 Franklin Watts

First published in Great Britain
    1990 by
Franklin Watts
96 Leonard Street
London EC2A 4RH

First published in the USA by
Franklin Watts Inc
387 Park Avenue South
New York
NY 10016

First published in Australia by
Franklin Watts
14 Mars Road
Lane Cove
NSW 2066

UK ISBN: 0 7496 0304 6

A CIP catalogue record
for this book is available
from the British Library

Printed in Belgium

Designed by
K and Co

Photographs by
NASA
Anglo-Australian Telescope Board
Royal Observatory, Ediburgh
California Institute of Technology
US Naval Observatory
Armagh Planetarium

Technical Consultant
Brian Jones

Note – billion
The term billion in this book
has been used to indicate
1,000 million.

The Picture World of

Sun AND Stars

N. S. Barrett

CONTENTS

Franklin Watts

London • New York • Sydney • Toronto

Introduction

The Sun is a star. It is an average star, like billions of other stars in the universe. The Earth and the other planets revolve around the Sun.

Most stars belong to groups called galaxies. There are about 100 billion stars in our galaxy, which is sometimes called the Milky Way. There are billions of other galaxies in the universe.

The life of an average star like the Sun is 10 billion years. The Sun is about half-way through its life.

▽ The Sun is a fiery body, radiating huge amounts of heat and light every second. It is a mass of hydrogen and helium gases at very high temperatures.

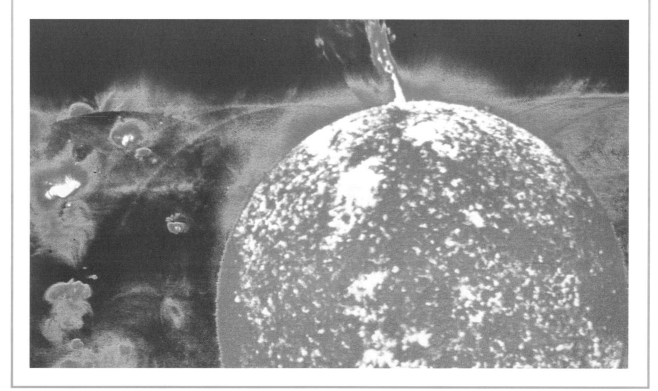

▷ A large telescope, used for studying the heavens. People who study the stars and other bodies in the universe are called astronomers.

▽ Stars as seen through a powerful telescope, which magnifies a small portion of the night sky.

7

The Sun in action

The Sun is like a huge furnace in space. Its fuel is hydrogen gas, the simplest of all substances.

At the heart of the furnace, hydrogen atoms come together at temperatures of millions of degrees. This causes nuclear fusion, as in the hydrogen bomb. Another gas, helium, is formed, and huge amounts of energy are produced.

This energy is gradually carried to the surface of the Sun, from where it escapes as heat and light.

▽ The Sun releases enormous amounts of energy into space. Only a small part of it reaches Earth. But it provides us with heat and light, and makes life on Earth possible.

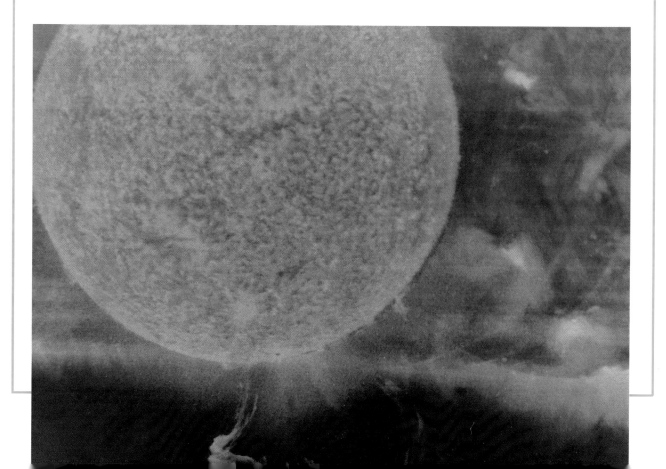

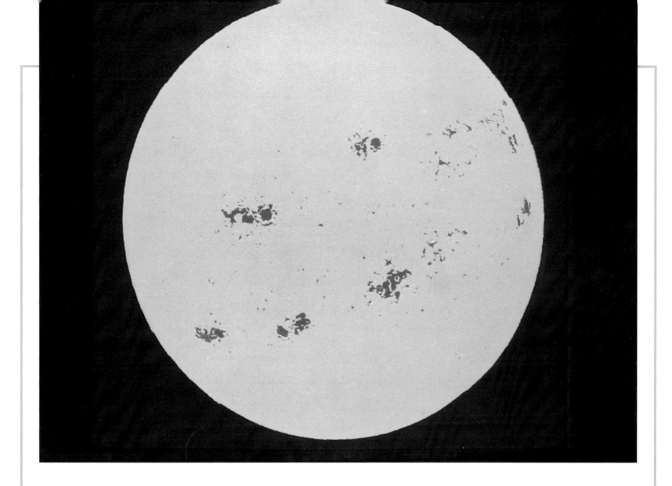

The core (centre) of the Sun is under tremendous pressure. So, although it contains only gases, it is more than 100 times as dense as water.

The temperature of the core is about 15,000,000°C. It gradually gets cooler towards the Sun's surface, which is 5500°C.

Patches may be seen on the Sun's surface that look darker than the rest of it. These are called sunspots. They look darker because they are at a lower temperature.

△ A photograph of sunspots made by an instrument that measures magnetism. Sunspots are caused by increased magnetism. They occur regularly on the Sun's surface and usually last for a few weeks. The number of sunspots varies, and about every 11 years reaches a maximum.

Violent events that take place on the surface of the Sun are called solar storms. These take the form of either bright bursts of light called flares, or huge arches of gas called prominences.

Solar storms are associated with sunspots, and are a result of magnetic forces. All this solar activity can affect weather and radio communications on Earth.

△ Great loops of hot gases on the Sun's surface are steered by the magnetism of the Sun.

▷ This photograph of the Sun shows one of the most spectacular prominences ever recorded. It spanned 590,000 km (367,000 miles) across the Sun's surface – nearly 50 times the diameter of Earth.

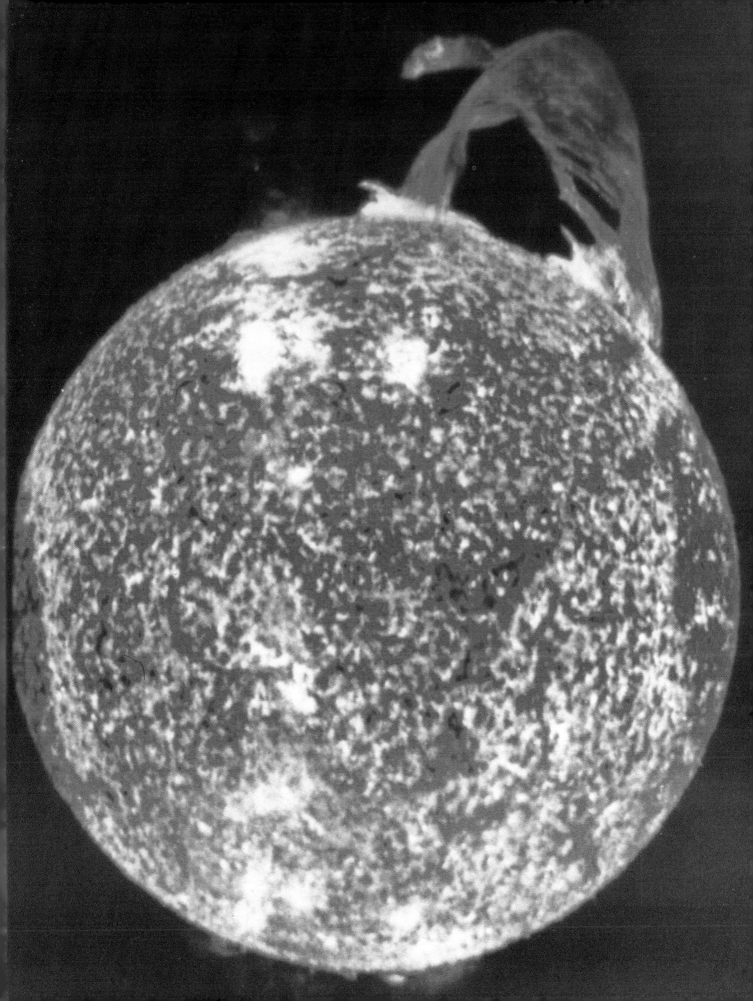

The distance from the centre to the surface of the Sun is 696,000 km (432,000 miles). Outside the core, the Sun becomes less dense. The surface, or photosphere, is only 550 km (340 miles) thick and may be thought of as the first layer of the Sun's atmosphere.

The temperature of the Sun's atmosphere climbs rapidly in the chromosphere, the middle layer, and the corona, the outer layer, where it reaches 2,000,000°C.

▽ This picture was made up from information received from a satellite sent up to study the Sun. It shows how the corona, the outer layer of the atmosphere, extends from the surface of the Sun. The colours are not true colours, but represent the density of the corona, from deep blue (densest) to yellow (least dense).

Eclipse of the Sun

In the sky, the Sun looks the same size as the Moon. This is because it is nearly 400 times as far away from Earth. When the Moon passes between the Sun and Earth, it completely blocks out the Sun's light. This is called a solar eclipse.

△ A total eclipse of the Sun. The Moon has completely covered the Sun's disk (the part we see in the sky) to reveal the corona. It is only during an eclipse that the Sun's corona becomes visible from Earth.

13

The night sky

On a clear night, about 3,000 stars can be seen with the unaided eye. Ancient astronomers divided the sky into groups of stars called constellations. We still use these groups today to map the sky.

Some stars look brighter than others. The brightness of a star from Earth depends not only on its true brightness, but also on its distance from Earth.

▷ A small portion of the sky as seen with a powerful telescope.

▽ The constellation of Ursa Major, or the Great Bear. The ancient scientists gave descriptive names to the groups of stars, imagining they saw them as shapes in the sky. This drawing also shows the Big Dipper, or Plough, joined by blue lines.

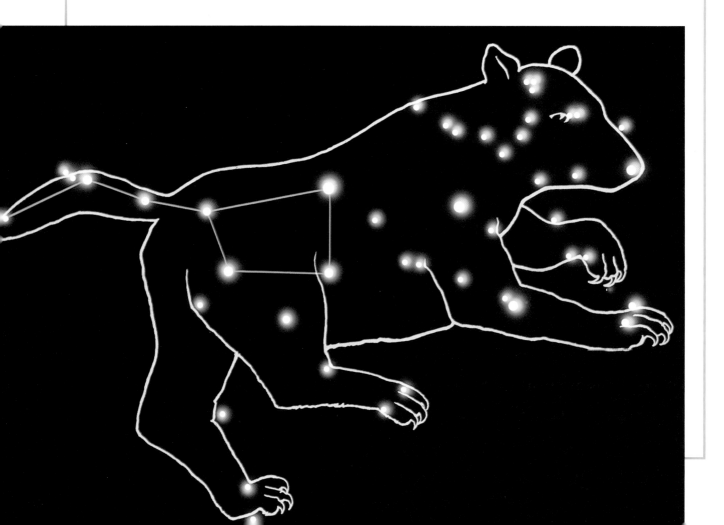

15

Every night the stars seem to move slowly across the sky. But this is only because the Earth itself is spinning. The stars are so far away that from one year to the next they are in the same position in the sky.

The stars we see in the night sky are all in our galaxy. The stars in a constellation are not a true group in the heavens. They only appear to be close together. From another part of the galaxy, they would make different patterns.

△ A long-exposure photograph shows how the stars appear to move across the sky. It is the slow, apparent movement of the sky as the Earth spins round that produces the star trails shown here. On short-exposure photographs, stars appear as points of light.

▷ A star cluster as seen through a powerful telescope. Clusters are groups of stars packed close together as they move through space.

▽ Telescopes reveal all kinds of strange and colourful shapes in the sky. This is the Horsehead Nebula. A nebula is a cloud of gas and dust in space.

17

Birth and death of stars

Stars vary according to their age and size. They are born out of great clouds of gas and dust in space.

Particles come together, drawn by the force of gravity. They form a globule which gets bigger and bigger, before slowly collapsing inwards under its own weight to become smaller and hotter.

This small, hot body, or protostar, pulls in more gas and dust. It gets so hot and dense that nuclear fusion begins to take place at its centre.

▽ The Great Nebula in the constellation of Orion. It is from such clouds of gas and dust as this that stars are born.

The outward acting force of heat from the nuclear reactions inside the star stops the collapse. The body begins to radiate heat and light. It is now a star.

Stars like the Sun shine for 10 billion years before their hydrogen runs out. They swell to 100 times their size to become red giants.

The outer layers are then shed to leave a central core that collapses into a white dwarf. This gradually gets cooler and its light dies out.

▽ The Ring Nebula in the constellation of Lyra. This is a different kind of nebula. It was formed when a dying star shed its outer layer. The star itself is now collapsing into a white dwarf.

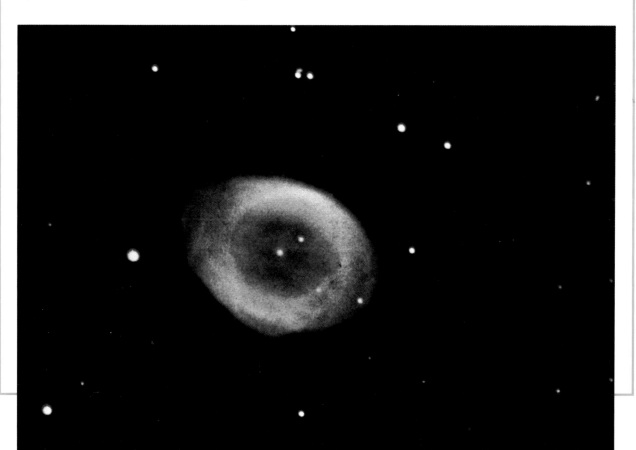

Galaxies

The vast amount of space occupied by a galaxy is very difficult to imagine. In our galaxy, the nearest star to the Sun is 40 million million km away. It takes light from this star 4.3 years to reach us. In the measure used by astronomers, it is 4.3 light-years away. Our galaxy is 100,000 light-years across.

Our galaxy has a spiral shape, with arms of stars coiling out from the centre. Some galaxies are elliptical (oval).

△ A view towards the centre of our galaxy. It is not hard to see why it is called the Milky Way. Great clouds of dust blot out the light from many stars, although these stars can still be detected by radio waves.

▷ The Andromeda Galaxy is the farthest object in the night sky that can be seen with the unaided eye. It is more than 2 million light-years away.

△ A spiral galaxy showing clearly how the arms coil out from a central bulge, like a vast rotating catherine wheel in space.

◁ A giant elliptical galaxy, about 50 million light-years away. This one, which is almost round, is 20 times the size of an average galaxy like the Milky Way.

Galaxies are usually found in groups. It is difficult to appreciate how things millions of light-years apart can belong to the same group. But in the vastness of the universe, there are millions of these clusters of galaxies, ranging in size from a few members to thousands.

Our group of galaxies has about 30 members. The nearest to us are two small galaxies called the Magellanic Clouds, nearly 200,000 light-years away.

△ A group of galaxies about 55 million light-years distant. The one in the top right corner is clearly a spiral galaxy. Most of the others that can be seen are elliptical. These range in shape from spherical, like a tennis ball, to flattened like a rugby ball.

Studying the stars

Anyone can study the stars. On a clear night, you can make out many of the constellations and identify the brightest stars. A pair of good binoculars or a small telescope will enable you to see very much more.

Astronomers study the heavens from observatories, with large telescopes. They observe and measure radio and other waves from the stars as well as light.

▷ The big dome of an observatory opens at night to allow the telescope to study the heavens. For observing or photographing objects in the sky, the telescope moves round at the same speed as the Earth is spinning.

▽ Computers control the motions of the dome and telescope.

Facts

Size of the Sun
The Sun measures about 1,392,500 km (865,000 miles) across. This is about 109 times the diameter of the Earth. About 1.3 million Earths would fit into the Sun.

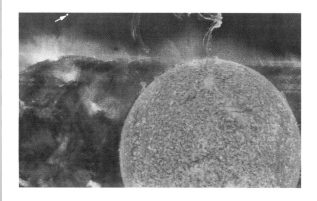

△ The size of the Earth compared with the Sun is shown by the white dot arrowed at the top left of the picture. If the Sun were hollow, it would hold more than a million Earths.

Distance of the Sun
The Earth orbits the Sun in a slightly elliptical path, so it is not always the same distance away. The average distance between Earth and Sun is about 150 million km (93 million miles). It takes light from the Sun about 8 minutes 20 seconds to reach Earth.

The size of stars
A white dwarf might be only half as big as the Earth, whereas some supergiants are 1,000 times the size of the Sun.

An average star
The Sun is an average star, about half-way through its life. It is made up mainly of the simplest elements, the gases hydrogen (73%) and helium (25%).

Nearest star
The nearest star to our Solar System is Proxima Centauri, a faint red dwarf. This is one of a group of three stars all about 4.3 light-years from the Sun, a distance of 40 million million km (25 million million miles).

Dwarfs
Stars like the Sun become white dwarfs near the end of their life. These are amazingly heavy for their size, weighing as much as the Sun yet perhaps no bigger than Earth. When a white dwarf has radiated the last of its energy, it becomes a black dwarf the

size of a planet and no longer shines like a normal star.

A red dwarf is a star much smaller than the Sun and only just big enough for nuclear fusion to occur at its core. Red dwarfs burn their fuel slowly and give out comparatively little light. But they last much longer than the Sun, up to a million million years.

Giants
Average stars like the Sun swell up after billions of years to become red giants before they die out.

Even larger than the red giants are the brilliant, hot supergiants. These start out as large stars, much bigger than the Sun. But they have a relatively short life, perhaps only a few million years. They expand into even larger red supergiants before they die.

Brightest star
The brightest star in our night sky is Sirius, 8.7 light-years away. Also known as the Dog Star, it lies in the constellation of Canis Major.

Exploding stars
Stars larger than the Sun burn out more quickly. A star 10 times as heavy as the Sun burns out in a hundredth of the time. Some very massive stars collapse at the end of their lives and are destroyed in a huge explosion called a supernova. The light from a supernova can equal that given out by the stars of an entire galaxy.

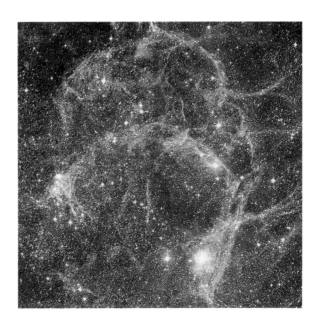

△ The remains of a supernova explosion in the constellation of Vela about 12,000 years ago. On exploding, the star would have become 100 million times as bright as the Sun, and rivalled the Moon in our night sky.

27

Glossary

Constellation
A named group of stars by which astronomers find their way about the night sky. There are 88 officially recognized constellations.

Core
The centre of a star, in which nuclear fusion takes place.

Corona
The outer layer of the Sun's atmosphere.

Eclipse
The blocking out of one body in the sky by another crossing its path. A solar eclipse is when the Moon blocks out the Sun.

Galaxy
A huge collection of billions of stars, dust and gas.

Light-year
The distance travelled by light in a year.

Nebula
A cloud of gas and dust in space from which new stars are formed.

Nuclear fusion
The process that takes place in the core of stars when hydrogen is turned into helium with a massive release of energy.

Red dwarf
A small, long-lived, faint star.

Red giant
A star that has swollen to a great size when its hydrogen fuel has almost run out.

Solar
To do with the Sun.

Sunspot
An area on the surface of the Sun that appears dark because it is not as hot as its surroundings.

Supernova
An explosion following the collapse of a very massive star.

White dwarf
A very small and very dense star that has used up its nuclear energy and is near the end of its life.

Index

29